MY HOME AND CAREER:

GUIDE ON HOW TO BALANCE YOUR HOME AND CAREER.

BY

B. O EMMA

TABLE OF CONTENTS

INTRODUCTION

Each man wants quietness and a small portion of etiquette around them. When you consider "Home" following a long, occupied, distressing day at work, or when your chief or a collaborator is making you insane, what pictures come into view? In this writing, "Home" is characterized as having three essential characteristics: wellbeing, solace, and quietness. These are the advantages of having an actual design you can call "Home." It offers genuine serenity, insurance from weather conditions, dangers, security, and individual wellbeing. It likewise makes a quiet and charming environment. What spurs a man to get back is the satisfaction that comes from having a need met. The advantages of getting back every day hold him back from leaving.

Each man will continuously need to return home to an intriguing and carefree spouse. As indicated by late perceptions and speculations, there are a few key things that men love to have, and that will be regarded, required, and satisfied. A lady's qualities will decide if she will give this to the man and make him anticipate getting back to her every day. A man will continuously find solace in his lady's arms once she gives him all that he wants. Does he track down such satisfaction with you?

A delightful woman is content and certain about herself No one loves somebody poor, uncertain, or gripping. Man will see this as exceptionally appalling. Being a sure woman with a solid identity is hot. Ladies are less unconstrained than guys, as per studies, yet men especially appreciate being spontaneous. The ladylike orientation has the regular need to feel secured, extraordinary, and wanted. Men revere it when a lady loosens up and embraces impulsivity. So now is the right time to allow him to amaze you, and if you can, he'll see the value in it too. Try not to be a little careful the least bit!

A decent man truly wants the chance to satisfy a lady. To have the feeling that he can give you anything you require and that you won't have to go somewhere else for affection or consideration. Thc man carncstly wants to be your sparkling knight! Permitting him to satisfy you is the key! Men appreciate the feeling required in a decent close-to-home sense. It is a paradox to imagine that since ladies are achieved and wise, men aren't attracted to them.

Men long for the ideal lady as they age. They search for the qualities in another person that they appreciate and observe. They play a long and hazardous game in light of their swelled assumptions. In any case, eventually, what they need is love. Men begin to recognize the insights and lies of what they realized as they go. As their collaborations and encounters progress, they step by step let go of their expanded assumptions. Life turns into a fresh start ready to be loaded up with our actual longings. They all want love since they think it restores them.

This assumption for persevering through affection is imbued in them from early on. We likewise require an objective. There won't likely ever be an "answer" to the all-inclusive existential inquiries that involved Socrates and Whitman, one that fulfills all of us. Men, in the interim, long for a reaction. They wish to be where they fit in. Since it isn't WHAT they do yet HOW what they do causes them to feel that is important, that spot could be downtown from their home where they work. Think about existence as an excursion along a waterway of sentiments. Where life is not set in stone by the close-to-home stream. We are creatures that follow our feelings.

There is dependably a vacuum inside, says the man. Each man has a reason to satisfy which is principal to their reality. Have you seen the association between the objective we have and the affection we want? A man should have a justification behind his reality. A man is cheerful when he finds his main goal and has somebody who truly cherishes him. Hell, a man's just objective in life can be to be loved! The universe made every one of us as per a similar example, yet with tremendously different materials. We see life from an alternate layered vantage point, with stunningly changed experience calculations and life understandings. Notwithstanding, the very wonderfulness that made us ties us together.

A man is cheerful when he finds his calling and has somebody who truly cherishes him. Hell, a man's just objective in life can be to be preferred! The universe made every one of us as indicated by a similar example, yet with immensely different materials. We see life from an alternate layered vantage point, with ridiculously changed experience calculations and life translations. Nonetheless, the very superbness that made us ties us together. Men are undeniably filled with the craving to be perfect. At the point when they see it, they at the same time appreciate and ache for it. Their longing to be incredible is a consequence of this essential profound reaction.

Men need to issue, all things considered, by the day's end. We need to be somebody's legend around evening time and Clark Kent during the day. Being the legend of your darling is the best inclination on the planet. There is only one thing passed on to do if she cherishes you and offers you an objective:

CHAPTER ONE

Marriage is a relationship between two grown-ups of the other gender, each soul mate in a marriage has commitments he/she wants to fulfill for the association to run true to form. Sidestepping liabilities by mates is one of the huge supports for why connections miss the mark.

Along these lines, you are getting hitched! Contemplating what the positions of a mate in a family are? We take care of you. In the past, most companions remained at home to do family assignments, care for young people, and manage the family. As of now, women are breaking those predispositions! A life partner isn't by and large dedicated to staying at home. Women these days are pursuing their occupations. Today, men understand the need to contribute to tasks and family endeavors. With everything taken into account, what are the commitments of a life partner in the present social quirks? In this article, we separate the positions and commitments of a companion in marriage.

Marriage changes the presence of a woman; from a ruined happy young woman, she forms into a careful mate ready to expect the commitments of a spouse. We ought to figure out the thing those commitments are: Expecting you have any time sewn a dress or tried to sew one, you know how a model works. The model is made of many pieces, some colossal and some little, none of which exactly seem to be the finished thing. Right when you spread out the model and cut the texture, you don't have a garment yet only a couple of bits of material. Right when it is properly gathered and made usable with buttons, snaps, or a zipper, these pieces make an all-out dress. Every model has sets of parts: two sleeves, two bodice pieces, a front, and back skirt, and, shockingly, the collar and defying pieces are, generally speaking, in twos. Marriage is similar. Correspondingly, a dress can be made in a collection of sizes and assortments with different differences comprehensively from one model, so my marriage could seem, by all accounts, to be special from yours.

As we perceive Christ as the Expert in our lives, we ought to figure out our connections as demonstrated by God's course of action. The key is for each mate to stay on course, know her part, and work to track down a spot with her significant other's liabilities. The occupation of a companion in marriage is major to bring motivation and keep the family more grounded. Life partners need love, compassion, care, respect, and support from their huge other to extend their limits and achieve life goals. Your friendship and support can be his power. Most women take care of family commitments and consideration and tutoring their adolescents. You could stay aware of your balance and poise while zeroing in on your soul mate and family. It is also essential to save valuable open doors for yourself and achieve your life targets.

A solid mate helps a man with extending his limits, achieving his dreams, and making genuine progress all through day-to-day existence. So what exactly is the occupation of a mate in a man's life? A nice life partner drives positive changes in a man. During challenges, she remains right by him, empowering him in affection. She manages the children and administers all that at home, autonomously. She is a multi-tasked who directs work and home with precision. This book uncovers and gives you the right view concerning the work a companion plays in a man's life and why she is vital to her friends and family.

More than later ever, women today need an undeniable cognizance of how they should associate with their life partners. The basic social changes accomplished by women's opportunity advancement all through ongoing numerous years have provoked such chaos that the general idea of "obligation" is hostile to some. They feel like somehow they lose their personality and their chance of accepting they adhere to some kind of "outdated standard."

CHAPTER TWO

Obligations OF A Decent Spouse

Real Closeness

The term 'wifely commitment' is indivisible from a mate requiring sex in a marriage. Beholding back to the 20s and 50s, mates should be accessible to take part in sexual relations at whatever point with their better half. It was their 'wifely commitment' that went with being hitched. Anyway, things of factors to consider concerning genuine closeness and marriage. The typical error is that women don't require sex once they get hitched. Women have been raised with the likelihood that they ought to be consistent, and that sex is fundamental for the satisfaction of men. Customarily, criticized for being open about their sexuality. Excessively basic terms, in a general sense female-gendered, are oftentimes used to portray wantonness. Society demands that women be genuinely appealing yet not caring about. However, today, women are embracing their sexuality. The likelihood that a woman's sexual satisfaction changes once she transforms into a mate is old.

Women should be ruined. Marriage doesn't give the mate a free right to sex anytime. "A man may be the highest point of the family, yet a woman is a neck and she can turn the head in any event needs" Exploration shows that the longer couples have been together, the lesser sex they will by and large have

(1). Another audit showed that the conflicting course of family tasks could cripple women before the day's finished and cause them not to incline toward sex

(2). Women should cook, clean, do the apparel, and work an entire day calling, while most mates work at work and don't be guaranteed to help with the family assignments. Close by these comes the commitment of managing the youths - that there is no huge astonishment that women are exhausted and have to rest continuously.

Now and again, women are genuinely repressed and oftentimes feel embarrassed to tell their accessories what gives them sexual satisfaction. This makes them unsatisfied, and sex regularly transforms into a task for them. Another crediting variable to the decrease in sexual development of inmates is their lessening interest in a fast in and out. At the point when you were dating, taking part in sexual relations was energizing and pleasant. You appreciated eliminating each other's articles of clothing and quitting any funny business. Nevertheless, as women age, the prerequisite for ensured sexual fulfillment decreases. Foreplay transforms into a big deal here! Have a go at giving your soul mate a back rub - it can in like manner be just a norm back rub to ease the heat off. Cut out the potential chance to ruin your soul mate and show her the sum she means to you.

Women, you don't simply engage in sexual relations when you would prefer not to. Quite a long time ago, mates believed it to be their commitment to fulfill their spouses truly regardless of when they would rather not. As of now, things are interesting. Ladies, let your life partner know whether you would rather not participate in sexual relations. Sex transforms into an errand on the off chance that you participate in it just to fulfill your life partner.

Regardless, remember that men will commonly be more physical.

They need genuine closeness. While it is OK to not be there of the brain for sex, there may be an issue assuming you never want to participate in sexual relations. This doesn't suggest that you want to propel yourself to have sex with your assistant. Taking everything into account, require a day to over-indulge yourself, basically, loosen up, or chill at the spa - and subsequently, get comfortable with your associate.

Cut out the chance to get into the attitude for sex. Be open to talking with specialists who can offer you heading on the best technique to prepare things up. Life partners, accepting that you feel unfulfilled, let your accessory in on what works for you. Surrender the disgrace that goes with being open about your sexual desires. Being open, a mate needs her life partner's consideration, and a spouse needs his significant other's. Appear for him when he wants to banter with you. Focus on him and guide him at whatever point required, and manage his necessities. It shows that you love and care for him.

CHAPTER THREE

Equality

In any relationship, equality is central. Dispose of the jumbled thought that one ought to understand what different think and need. Talking with your life accomplice should not be troublesome. It should not be stacked up with shock, disillusionment, fighting, and warmed conflicts. It should be tomfoolery and something you expect.

Your soul mate can't figure out minds, correspondingly as you can't. You may know all about every other's decisions and inclinations yet not what they are thinking or feeling. Open equality in the marriage suggests that you let your significant other in on what you think or feel and what you expect of him. Chat with your soul mate - ask, say, and discuss. Avoid calm treatment, which can worsen what is happening. Make an effort not to leave your life partner guessing about what you want. It will be more brilliant to clear your cerebrum, endeavor to figure out what you genuinely need while being direct to yourself, and a short time later grants that to him.

Make time for conversations that include what you love about one another and are doing great towards one another when you need to talk as well as placing into thought his preparation to need such conversations, examine your damages and how you can determine them, and your apprehensions too. While having such conversations, don't be on the edge side however, tune in with persistence and be remorseful should if you're at any shortcoming.

Play is one action that enchants a man and captivates them into a more profound level of "connection." Men appreciate playing and being dynamic. They were educated to utilize Activities to articulate their thoughts and make associations with others around them. Sadly, a ton of ladies seem to have failed to remember this and are attempting to prevail upon a man by talking, talking, talking. Nonetheless, truly given what you SAY, men don't "feel it" for you. It's the experience, not the words.

Getting things done with him will build your appeal to him. You can watch or play sports with him, contend in games like ping pong, and even add some prodding and mockery here and afterward.

Respect

Respect is normal. Regard his viewpoints and respect him for what he is. Expecting that you can't resist the urge to go against him, don't ignore him anyway, and put across your point carefully. Right when you give respect, you gain appreciation. Whenever you respect your significant other you love him, notice him, regard him, honor him, incline toward him, and respect him. It infers his perspective, regarding his knowledge and character, appreciating his commitment to you, and contemplating his necessities and values.

Our companions have a few necessities. Keep his honor/regard. Try not to discuss your significant other with your family, friends, or relatives. Do whatever it takes not to contend with him or question his position before others. Make an effort not to appreciate gabbing about your life partner. Expecting you have any issues, sort them out among yourselves. The macho man, who is free, independent, and invulnerable is a dream. At one event Walter furnished me with a summary of what he saw as a part of the fundamental necessities most men have: Valor in his hood as a man, to be focused on, Companionship, to be required or needed.

Addressing these prerequisites is the thing concerning your significant other. To help Dennis' sureness, for example, I endeavor to engage him by being his principal fan. Every life partner keeps up with that his soul mate ought to be in his gathering, to coach him when fundamental, but specifically to be his group advertiser. A mate needs a spouse who is behind him, really trusts him, appreciates him, and supports him as he goes out into the world reliably

Numerous ladies embrace the bogus presumption that men are looking for a "more fragile" lady who will cause them to feel more clever and solid. Nothing is more misleading than it is. A woman who rouses them is attractive to Genuine MEN since she is encountering progress in her own life.

They want a woman who isn't simply keen on connections yet in addition has her objectives. Tragically, a ton of ladies seem to have failed to remember this and are attempting to TALK their direction into a man's heart. In any case, in all actuality despite what you SAY, men don't "feel it" for you. Achievement and opportunity don't "threaten" a man. A man esteems the accompanying:

On the off chance that a man is attracted to a lady, a circumstance will ultimately emerge where you and the man will see things diversely and misconstrue each other. How might you answer this and offer your considerations? A lady with the development to not censure or scrutinize somebody for their activities

CHAPTER FOUR

Love

One of the commitments of a decent spouse is to revere Love him unequivocally: In a marriage, a man should be respected, esteemed, and esteemed as much as a woman should be. As a companion, give unhindered love to your soul mate really and internally. Esteem him generously and support him as your child. Furthermore, what do you get subsequently? His authentic love.

Love, they say, is the best of all. I encourage spouses "to esteem their husbands." A fair depiction of the kind of love your soul mate necessities is "certified affirmation." all things considered, recognize your better half in much the same way as he is — a flawed person. Love moreover suggests being centered on a usually fulfilling sexual relationship. I comprehend there is something else to love besides sex, notwithstanding, we are looking at how to fulfill God's structure to value our life partners. Thus, we ought to look at fondness as per their perspective, notwithstanding our own.

Concentrates on showing that sex is one of a man's most critical prerequisites — if not the most huge. Whenever a mate goes against closeness, is uninterested, or is simply inertly interested, her significant other could feel excused. It will cut at his psychological self-representation, tear at him to the genuine focal point of his being, and make withdrawals. My soul mate's sexual necessities should be more huge and higher on my need list than menus, housework, assignments, works out, and, shockingly, the children. It doesn't suggest that I should contemplate sex the whole day and reliably, yet it suggests that I track down approaches to remembering my life partner and his necessities. It suggests I save a part of my energy for him. This keeps me away from being prideful and living only for my necessities and requirements. Staying aware of that middle helps me with beating segregation in our marriage.

Give space for certain blemishes and figure out how to disregard his mix-ups. Practice tolerance, love shows restraint. Persistence comes easily. It is alright to toss in pleasant commendations to your soul mate. Try not to continuously zero in on his shortcomings and accentuate them. Right when you are playing out numerous undertakings reliably with your commitments at home, and things don't go as you plan, the last thing you consider is resilience. Regardless, make a pass at having it and you won't mull over it. Imagine, that you are eager to compete to work, your significant other asks you something silly and you influence him. Anyway, later in the day, you comprehend that he was just endeavoring to be carefree with you. Had you been more comprehensible close to the start of the day, the day would have been remarkable both for yourself as well as your better half.

Help him, who said men don't need support? They all need help and sponsorship. Loan some assistance during troublesome stretches. At the point when he searches for your help, be proactive in supporting him. He will do the same when you want his assistance.

Accommodation

Everybody should comprehend the idea of the utilization of a manual of "something" being made to have the option to bridle the principal reason for why "that thing" was made. The possibility of accommodation in marriage has a long history and is imbued in male-centric culture. The assumption that a lady submits to her significant other is normally severe since countless men have gripped to the accommodation language to get male matchless quality in marriage; it is a round of force and control. Some supportive of orientation uniformity Christian with the destructive orientation equity developments that plan to legitimize all types of male hawk the Good book orders ladies to submit to their spouses. Is it problematic to help orientation equity while likewise upholding the subjection of ladies in marriage? Does Christianity energize ladies as objects of accommodation? Does submitting infer being oppressed? Is submitting alright?

Marriage accommodation doesn't involve servitude or driving a lady to surrender her independence; rather, it includes magnanimity, administration, responsibility, and regard for your companion, which should all be equal. The foundation of Christian marriage is endlessly loving is anything aside from the longing to be in control.

Wives ought to approach their mates with deference as opposed to in an easygoing way.

Never should spouses treat their husbands as though they are quitters. A few companions disregard their spouses' thoughts or proclamations or even intrude on their husbands. They dismiss his guidance and administration as though they were immaterial. A few women are forceful and battle with their spouses constantly. They give him the feeling that he is ceaselessly lacking. They persistently right him and debate with him as though he is unequipped forever figuring things out. As indicated by Sayings 19:13, a spouse's battle resembles a storm that won't ever stop. The Holy book deserves spouses to admiration their husbands, subsequently, when they treat them nonchalantly, they are defying that order.

A spouse ought to have a "conscious and unadulterated way of behaving," as indicated by 1 Peter 3:2. Obviously, a spouse can delicately offer her viewpoints to her significant other. She may graciously contradict him too. The contemplations and inner voice of a spouse don't have a place with the husband. She should, notwithstanding, continually regard him. Two people will not be walking together for extremely lengthy on the off chance that they have separate spots to reach. The two of them should choose a similar objective to remain together. In any case, what happens when two individuals are out walking and start to disagree regarding where to go? They can't keep on strolling together except if one of them respects the other. Relationships should stay accommodating to one another. There should be accommodation. The spouse will either give up to the husband, or the husband will submit to the wife.

CHAPTER FIVE

A Career Lady and a Spouse: Find some kind of harmony.

Changing the solicitations of an errand, an individual life, a mechanized life (i.e., the everyday intrusion of messages, messages, and posts), and a serious relationship can weaken. Legitimate, it's endlessly out a ton once in a while. Every so often, tapping out can seem like the more straightforward way.

Our high-level lives explicitly are adding new tensions to our affiliations. In case your relationship is battling, your friend's online diversion post showing pictures from a resulting unique first night can leave you feeling done for and disheartened. "You'll ask yourself, forgetting briefly that posts using virtual amusement are a significant part of the time filtered through rose-concealed central focuses. Undeniably more horrible, you could wind up in a shame curving: "How do various couples get it going, while we're engaging? Why aren't we better at this? Coming up next are five clues to help you with doing exactly that.

Diminish Normal Uproar

Eliminating the dull sound of your life is no straightforward task. It requires evaluating your scene and subsequently influencing change. Nonetheless, especially like during spring cleaning, discarding things can be hard — if not, our closets wouldn't be jam-stacked with ten-year-old sweaters that at this point don't fit. We're hesitant to quit any pretense of, asking ourselves, "Envision a situation in which I need that.

For twofold capable couples especially, normal dreary sounds feel like that load of old sweaters. In a mentioning position, it's for the most part expected to feel "ready and waiting" reliably, on the occasion, some startling need arises. For a couple of us, it's challenging to perceive that we're consuming resources — be this present time is the ideal open door, energy, or storeroom space — on "what vulnerabilities." Resources that could be redirected into our connections.

Directing foundation commotion, and the huge number of smaller than usual solicitations that go with it is a basic piece of a strong relationship. Whether it's toning down on how quickly you answer messages, limiting your experience on capable web diaries, turning off your phone after nine o'clock, or even de-zeroing in on a connection you've outgrown, finally, you'll have extra time and focus to accommodate your relationship.

Center around Your Relationship

Anyone in a serious association has heard that continuing on articulation, "Associations take work!" And it's legitimate, no sound relationship runs on autopilot. There's no staying away from it: To save your marriage, you ought to zero in on it.

Notwithstanding different things, zeroing in on suggests you ought to continually save several gallons in your gas tank for your mate. Whether or not you're canine tired when you get back after working all day, require two or three minutes to check in with your assistant. "Zeroing in on" implies you do this whether or not your serious arrangement neglected to work out, whether or not you're facing an immeasurable deadline, or in any case whether your boss blamed you after lunch.

Office concerns can send anyone's head swimming, in any case, they're not a valid justification for neglecting to get a few data about your friend's day and the fights they defied. These conversations, paying little heed to how short, will keep you and your accessory related notwithstanding mentioning agonies of your positions.

Truly resolve to Clear Liabilities — and Keep Them

Expecting that you have an unprecedented arrangement for finishing work, intentional, cautious supporting of your relationship is major. You ought to remove time for your mate and defend that time. Center around a film night one time each week, a month-to-month evening out on the town, or a quarterly week's end escape. Anything that procedures you pick, this is the ideal chance for yourself as well as your life accomplice just; it's a chance to relax, reconnect, and esteem being with each other.

There's some serious fine print that appears with liabilities: they ought to be kept. Right when life is pulling you in 1,000 headings immediately, it's unreasonably easy to permit things to get away from everybody's notification. Your marriage, notwithstanding, isn't one of these things. Be capable of your accessory: if you can't keep an obligation, it's on you to reschedule as a way to deal with zeroing in on your marriage. It's alright to occasionally move a night out to one more booked space to oblige your over-arranged life, yet it's not confirming to disregard.

Convey Improvement to Your Affection

For sure, you're involved. Particularly involved. It makes perfect sense to us, we get it. However, paying little mind to how troubling your occupation is, your buddy is a piece of your heart and cerebrum, whether or not your spotlight right currently is on the report you're presenting. Regardless, after you've nailed that show (and after you've taken a full breath), quickly making the most of an open door or two to assist your assistant with recollecting your companionship can colossally influence your relationship. Besides, even though old age brings explicit challenges, it also simplifies it than any time in ongoing memory to show your appreciation and love for your associate.

Demand your life accomplice an unforeseen lunch using your #1 menu application. Email an article about a showcase you should see together. Shoot off a text with an inside joke. Send a selfie with "Missing you" in the caption. These movements shouldn't mess around with too clear or incredible — and they shouldn't be. The truth of the matter is showing your glow in little ways, regardless, when you're not together. A clear, "I'm thinking about you" is the gold you're later.

Esteem Right here and now

Accepting at least for now that you're like most twofold occupation couples, losing all ability to know east from west in time's hurricane is basic. Yet again August seems to jump straight into October… and when you rotate toward the sky, New Year's Day is around the corner. Anyway critical as your occupation is by all accounts, don't permit time to sneak past rapidly.

The ongoing holds the best approach to building a beautiful future, not a contrary strategy for getting around. Consistently, simply present yourself with this request, "What did I do today to communicate with my associate?" If you come up short, you need to contribute some piece more energy. Start immediately: banter with your buddy with interest and care. A bit "I'm tuning in" goes the distance. A hug never hurts, in light of everything. These little, in-the-present exhibitions create and continue with the relationship for a lengthy time.

Doubtlessly that our callings are huge. Other than financial occupation, our positions can offer us gigantic master satisfaction, and we put forth a strong attempt to achieve our goals. Anyway, work is never supported for ignoring a marriage, not regardless of when both of you are in high-pressure positions. While the troublesome activity can be inconvenient every so often, the genuine work is huge. By showing to your mate that you're taking part in your relationship and significantly committed to your affiliation, you're further developing the soil which your marriage creates.

CONCLUSION

Lastly, as per the Book of scriptures, love is the best of all.

Give all that it takes to work on your marriage and be the best companion you can be. Generally speaking, marriage is advantageous. make a deliberate move to encourage a strong climate for each other in your home. You will encounter the needs and assumptions you are expecting in your marriage when you depend on God for the solidarity to do the vast majority.

www.ingramcontent.com/pod-product-compliance
Lightning Source LLC
LaVergne TN
LVHW052112160826
845678LV00015B/3509